THE MAGIC
OF CHOOSING *UNCERTAINTY*

HOW TO MANAGE CHANGE,
EMBRACE FEAR
AND LIVE A FULFILLED LIFE

BY
TOM SCARDA

Tom Scarda
3404 Homestead Avenue
Wantagh, NY 11793
866-545-6191
Tom@TomScarda.com
www.TomScarda.com

Limits of Liability and Disclaimer of Warranty

The author and publisher shall not be liable for your misuse of this material. This book is strictly for informational and educational purposes.

Warning – Disclaimer

The purpose of this book is to educate and entertain. The author and/or publisher do not guarantee that anyone following these techniques, suggestions, tips, ideas, or strategies will become successful. The author and/or publisher shall have neither liability nor responsibility to anyone with respect to any loss or damage caused, or alleged to be caused, directly or indirectly by the information contained in this book.

In memory of my grandfather, Jack Piccininni, who chose uncertainty over unhappiness by immigrating from Italy to the United States of America where everyone has a chance to create his or her own reality.

Courage is resistance to fear, mastery of fear – not absence of fear.

–Mark Twain

I would like to thank my beautiful wife, Gina, for her undying support to this and all endeavors that my spirit calls forth.

To my parents, Joseph and Antoinette, thank you for deciding to bring me forth in 1963.

For Andrea and Anthony

Don't be afraid to take a big step if one is indicated. You can't cross a chasm in two small jumps.

–David Lloyd George

THE ROAD NOT TAKEN

By Robert Frost

Two roads diverged in a yellow wood,
And sorry I could not travel both
And be one traveler, long I stood
And looked down one as far as I could
To where it bent in the undergrowth;

Then took the other, as just as fair,
And having perhaps the better claim,
Because it was grassy and wanted wear;
Though as for that the passing there
Had worn them really about the same,

And both that morning equally lay
In leaves no step had trodden black.
Oh, I kept the first for another day!
Yet knowing how way leads on to way,
I doubted if I should ever come back.

I shall be telling this with a sigh
Somewhere ages and ages hence:
Two roads diverged in a wood, and I—
I took the one less traveled by,
And that has made all the difference.

NOTES TO READER

I have personally read hundreds of books, listen to countless cassette tapes, viewed innumerable compact discs and movies and attended a myriad of seminars. This book is the culmination of much of the data and material that I have been exposed to over the past two decades. At the end of this book I list the books that have had the most significant impact on me. I encourage you to seek out these publications and read them for yourself. The brilliant insights are freely given to us to help everyone lead a fulfilled life, regardless of their backgrounds.

The Fuel to Change

At key points in the book I will suggest techniques on how to harness and understand your fear, anxiety or apprehensions. I call these sections: **The Fuel to Change**.

The Fuel to Change sections are mostly exercises on paper. You don't have to do them. But I have found that putting intentions on paper is powerful and the *power* you will harness by following through with the exercises in this book is the authentic FUEL TO CHANGE.

TABLE OF CONTENTS

INTRODUCTION

The stock markets tumble much faster than they climb. People stay in relationships that are unfulfilling or even dangerous. Workers labor in jobs they hate. Prescriptions for controlling the symptoms of depression have skyrocketed. What gives?

In each of these examples, the driving force is FEAR!!!

In your life, you might have passed on a great business opportunity. You might have found the perfect partner, only to end the relationship because the fear of getting hurt was stronger than the idea of being happy. Or, perhaps you continue to toil at a job that leaves you unfulfilled, just to make ends meet.

When the phone rings at an unexpected hour do you automatically think it is bad news? What goes through your mind? When you're preparing for a road trip do you think there's going to be traffic? Do you turn on the radio news waiting to hear how bad the traffic backups are? Do you expect that your sniffles may turn into pneumonia?

Why does it seem that we are always expecting the worst? Is it inbred or do we actually attract our situations – good or bad? By the way, what is good and bad? Is it all about you? Could it be possible that you missing a red light means that someone else gets to his or her destination on time? Did that two-minute delay cause you to stand behind the old man at the lottery store causing you to receive the winning ticket instead of him? It is hard to know. But maybe, just maybe, there is something out there guiding all of us and if we just go with the flow we won't need to worry about a thing.

After all, we're all getting to the same place. And that place we came from gave us nothing, not a thing, no possessions and that's how we all will return. So why are we so hung up about getting to someplace?

These hang ups are what cause stress and worry to morph into real fear. We are told that if we lose that we are less. Fight for your rights. Fight for this and that. In this book I will examine and show you that you don't have to fight for anything because everything is in accordance with nature and the universe. And believe it or not, you can control much of it. You are creating in this very moment. Some are creating on purpose, but most are not. This book will address those who are not.

There is example after example of people who have moved passed their fears and live amazing lives filled with joy, peace and love. They start companies, run with a direct marketing concept or buy a franchise. Their relationships are solid and uplifting.

You can have this too...with a little work.

So, what is the difference between the happy people and the rest of society? Happy people have mastered the skills needed to evaluate, harness, embrace and eventually overcome even their deepest fears. They CHOOSE to focus on and give gratitude for what they have which ultimately brings more good stuff into their life.

In my book, you'll learn how fear works. You'll learn where your "fear center" is, how to identify legitimate fears and how to redefine the fears that keep you from all that you desire.

I certainly did, more than once, in many areas.

1

HOW YOUR MIND REALLY WORKS

Your mind is, by far, the most powerful tool at your disposal. Divided into two portions, your mind provides computing power for your life. Understanding how these portions interact with each other will help you understand where fears live and how to evaluate and overcome your fears. In upcoming chapters, you'll learn simple tips, tricks and exercises *or Fuel for your Change* by harnessing your own personal "computer." For now, let's get to know your mind.

Your mind is made up of two distinct parts: the conscious and the subconscious.

Your mind is like a global positioning satellite, GPS, in your car. To get from one place to another, from where you are to where you want to go – achieving your goals or your soul's desire, you need to program your mind. If you do not enter a destination in your GPS, it can only tell you where you are and not where you are going.

Your brain is the engine in your body, a lot like your car. Many of your body functions, including breathing, heartbeat, digestion and even the growing of your hair, are controlled by your brain and typically don't require conscious choice. Your brain works without your active involvement.

To be clear, the human brain or engine and the mind or GPS work independently of each other. The brain is not the topic of this book. The mind controls your decisions and thereby your life. The mind is what you need to understand and program to reach your destination. This will make all the difference in your life.

Your conscious mind functions without question, like a good soldier. If your conscious mind is told that you love pizza, it does not stop to evaluate the health benefits or risks of eating pizza. It simply sends messages throughout your body that pizza is good, allowing you to enjoy every bite. It's your subconscious mind that judges you for eating the pizza. It's not healthy, it's fattening and it goes right to your butt!

The problem with the mind is that it doesn't tell you that being afraid of spiders is probably silly, and that climbing onto the dinner table screaming at the sight of a small bug might be over the top. It just works, like a computer, with the programming it has been given.

To your conscious mind, nothing is good or bad, fun or scary, etc. Your conscious mind just plugs along, blissfully unaware that its reactions might not be the right thing for you.

Your subconscious mind, however, is where we get tripped up. Your subconscious mind is where memories and experiences are archived. It is also where your fears live. Once you learn how to control or correct programs in your subconscious mind, you will be able to harness its power to achieve whatever you want in your life.

Doctors often use teaching tools and exercises to help people overcome severe phobias. Phobias are often caused because of an abundance of poor programming in the subconscious mind coupled with an overreaction in the conscious mind. This is also the source of compulsions, addictions and other habits that might not be good for you.

Your subconscious mind is the accumulation of all of your experiences and education. It is amazing to watch how the subconscious mind is shaped and how the conscious mind will react to that shaping. Your subconscious mind is programmed by your experiences and how you react to them.

For example, imagine someone who is very overweight. Assuming that there are no legitimate health reasons for the obesity, the root cause of the extra pounds is flawed programming. A person who was told that they were fat as a child many times will program their subconscious to identify them as overweight. This label becomes their new "normal."

Since the conscious mind does not ask any questions, it will send signals to the person's body that they need to stay fat and therefore eat large quantities of unhealthy foods to maintain what the subconscious states as a "fact."

It is the same with fears. At some point or points in time, your conscious labels you as afraid of something. A simple example is a hot stove. Many children cannot help but touch a hot stove once as they explore their world. The immediate pain inputs data into the subconscious mind that hot stoves are not fun and should be avoided and even feared. In this example, the fear is appropriate and healthy.

But, what if your fear is not appropriate or healthy? Circling back to the overweight person, the original input might have come from a relationship failure. Perhaps someone they loved broke their heart. The subconscious mind might create programs to keep this person overweight in the hopes that they will avoid any future heartbreaks because they view themselves as less attractive. This is a good example of poor programming that can hold a person back from all they want. Even as the overweight person longs for someone to love them, their subconscious mind feels the need to protect them.

Everyone carries labels that they feel identify them. When you look in the mirror, what do you see? Are you attractive? Are you in good physical shape? Your impressions are coming from your subconscious mind and were forged throughout your life.

Ask yourself a few questions and you will start to see the programming that operates you. "What is my favorite food?" "What is my favorite color?" The answers to these were programmed into you, often during childhood.

Now, go a few steps deeper with some other questions. "Why did my past relationships fail?" "Why do I work at a job I hate?"

How might your programming about money affect you? If you have been programmed to believe that, "money is the root of all evil," or other similar programming, you would naturally avoid opportunities to add wealth to your life because you want to avoid the "evils," that wealth might bring.

This programming is sometimes explosive, but it is often more insidious. If a child is abused in some way, this explosive event will create programming that will almost certainly affect their future. But, consider a subtler example. As a child, you probably heard, as I did, an adult chide you to, "be careful," every time you left the house. Over time, this mantra could cause you to be overly cautious in all parts of your life.

Before we go further, I need to make an important point.

Generally speaking, there is no good or bad programming. I say this generally because if you carry programming that creates dangerous or unhealthy behaviors, these would probably be considered bad. BUT... YOU ultimately decide what is good or bad for you. As a human being, you get to decide what your life looks like.

The issue is when programing, that seemed harmless when received as a child, becomes a factor that is holding you back. For example, were you told that getting good grades in school will get you into a good college that will lead to a good job? There was no evil intent in teaching you that notion, but is it really true?

In my case, I knew that I did not want to work for anyone else, that I wanted a certain level of financial freedom and that I wanted time to enjoy other things in my life, including my family and hobbies. Some people around me thought I was crazy to think I could have it all. But, in the words of Forest Gump's mamma, "crazy is as crazy does" and I wouldn't trade my life for theirs, ever.

Programming, other than the dangerous kind, is left to you to evaluate, modify or support. The key point is that YOU are in the pilot's seat. You can reprogram and build whatever life you want, whenever you want it. You can actually reprogram your subconscious mind, but we need to add a couple more pieces to the puzzle before you begin.

First, I want to introduce you to a concept known as the Law of Attraction. I don't want to get too spooky here, but the Law of Attraction simply states that you will attract EXACTLY what your mind decides it wants. With one limitation that I will discuss in a moment, you can attract ANYTHING. In fact, you already do, and have been your entire life!

Think about the beloved cartoon character, Charlie Brown.

Charlie Brown had a little of all of us in him. He found it hard to enjoy life and often failed, yet his actions would lead you to believe he was the ultimate optimist. No matter how many times Lucy would lift the football just as Charlie Brown was going to kick it, he still believed that the next time she would keep the ball in place.

Charlie was not really an optimist. If you spend a lot of time with Charlie Brown, as his creator Charles Schultz did, you would notice that Charlie Brown believed that he would consistently fail, so he did. Charlie was ATTRACTING failure, because his subconscious mind had decided that he should fail.

On the other hand, no one would have been able to tell Lucy that she was going to fail at anything. More powerful than the confidence (almost arrogance) that she demonstrated was her subconscious belief that she would succeed. She was the queen of her kingdom and everyone around her should bow to her royalty. And they did!!!

There are two keys that defined these characters. First, what they BELIEVED to be true became their reality. But, second and equally important, the ACTIONS they took supported their belief.

Your subconscious is not susceptible to being tricked, either. People are often tripped up in their efforts to change their life because they try to use conscious thoughts to change subconscious programming. You can tell yourself you want to be wealthier until you are blue in the face, but nothing will change until you examine *your beliefs* about money and reprogram them to accept an endless supply of money as a tool in your life tool chest.

The Universe that swirls around us contains infinite possibility. Consider the achievements of man over time.

Our greatest achievements were a combination of belief and action, coupled with the boundless energy of the Universe. I capitalized Universe because I see it as a living being. If you are a religious person, you could insert "God" anytime I mention the Universe and you would be correct.

Do you need more proof? How does the wealth of the world continue to increase even though all resources, including money and natural resources should have a finite quantity? It is because we, the human race, are still tapping into the infinite wealth of the Universe around us.

Yet, the Law of Attraction operates at all times. As weird as it may sound, people are constantly attracting what their subconscious suggests they want. Many a dieter is tripped up in their efforts to lose weight because they keep telling the Universe that they want to lose weight. Don't blame the Universe for continuing to provide the weight to lose, as this is exactly what you requested!!!

But, the Universe is not a lottery. Your actions and your thoughts or dreams must be aligned. Simply wishing is not enough. The only magic lamp is your ability to connect your subconscious mind with your actions. In this reprogramming, you will see whatever it is that you want to see.

Most commonly, the process of *bending* the Universe to your will is known as manifesting. You manifest what you believe in your subconscious mind, using conscious thoughts and actions to support your desires.

Imagine how powerful you can become once you have the ability to reprogram your subconscious to deliver whatever you want at will.

But, there is one thing about the Universe that you need to know before you jump into rebooting your life. The Universe does not operate on your schedule. If you're religious, you have no doubt been taught that God wants the best for you and will deliver it to you in his own time. When we try to manipulate the Universe's clock, difficulty often occurs.

The way we handle what the universe delivers, even things and situations that are thought to be fantastic and life changing, depends greatly on how we were raised. People self-sabotage and set themselves back to where they began because of their beliefs about themselves. Many wonder if they are deserving of a great windfall and their lack of self-esteem may make them throw it all away.

How many lottery winners have lost their winnings within a few months? I'll bet you a million dollars that it was their education, beliefs and attitudes about money that cost them so much. Yet there are other winners that build more wealth with their lottery proceeds as a foundation. They have a healthy attitude about wealth, educate themselves about their financial options, see money as a tool for adding more wealth and support their beliefs with their spending habits and other actions. One has to be wealthy in his subconscious before he has wealth in his wallet.

The same is true about fears. Why do some people fear spiders and others love them. The spider lovers were probably never repeatedly told that spiders were dangerous and evil. They might have been shown how to properly handle spiders as a child. They could have read books about spiders in their free time and explored their surroundings in the hopes that they would meet a new spider. They view spiders as friends. Why would you not want to touch a friend?

The people who deeply fear spiders were programmed to fear them. A probable combination of education and experience taught them that spiders should be stomped or gassed at every opportunity. Maybe they saw a friend with symptoms of a severe spider bite or were bitten themselves. Most likely, they had a family member or members who hated spiders.

At a very young age, my older cousin, Donna who I looked up to as the older sister I never had, taught me to be scared of spiders and insects. As I grew into my own mind and was taken with the subject of science I realized insects, especially spiders are human's friends. They eat a lot of the stuff that is bad for us. As an adult I have trained myself and hopefully my children, to revere insects and spiders for what they contribute to our ecosystem.

I'm not suggesting that healthy caution is not appropriate as it relates to spiders, but rather demonstrating why two people can have such opposite reactions to a tiny creature. Neither reaction is good or bad. They are simply different.

2

THE THOUGHT PROCESS

Human brains are like complex computers. Information is input and stored. People become a memory bank of experiences and learned information. Like a computer, when a question is asked or a situation is approached, a person searches their memory banks for an answer or a similar experience. This information becomes a reaction for the person in the situation.

However, a human is more than a computer. We have the gift of thinking. If we ask a computer, "how can I build a personal hover craft?" The answer will not be available unless the information was previously uploaded. If you ask anyone the same question, most will not have the hover craft answer either, but one or two people will set out to figure build a personal hover craft. This is creating a new reality.

This is what makes human beings unique.

Unfortunately, when presented with a scenario, most people take the easy way out and query their memory banks or consult with a parent, teacher or clergy for answers. Most of the time, these people only regurgitate information that was passed down to them. However, some people, as rare as they are, will search their soul for a new or different idea.

Of course, taking a left when everyone else is going right is painful. Taking a chance to go outside of your comfort zone is challenging. But, therein lies the magic of human experience. All growth lays beyond our comfort zone.

For the person willing to break away from the crowd there is self-fulfillment. Do what the elders tell you to do, tried and true, and you get what they have gotten.

Instead of reliving the past, reach beyond your comfort zone, beyond what you have always done and create a new future for yourself.

I believe there are no wrong or right choices, just different incidents, occurrences, events and encounters that are ALL determined by your choices. Actually you can't lose!

As a summary to this chapter, I can tell you that human beings are not born with fears. You can dangle a spider over an infant for hours and the baby will only see the spider as interesting. So, fears are learned over time. Because you now know how fears start (outside programing) and where they live (in subconscious), you can begin to reprogram your life to overcome or dismiss the fears that are holding you back from your dreams.

Your dream, your passion, what your soul is calling you to do is God's plan, the plan of the Universe. Anything and everything you want is what your creator wants for you. After all, she put the idea in your mind to begin with. The problem is that you have had interference with your plans along the way. Our society, your parents, teacher, preachers and politicians tell you how you "should" live. You had no choice but to listen. They were older, and you believed, they must have known better.

In later years, you realize your elders didn't know anything. All they did was repeat what they had been told. But by then, it's often too late because their beliefs are now a part of you. Unless you detect what's happening, you will be caught in this useless cycle. However, with just a change in thought, you can make a positive impact on the world.

If you believe thought is extraordinarily powerful, you still only understand the half of it. Thought, attitude and faith are the keys to everything in life.

Thoughts are energy, just like television signals. You cannot see them but you know they are there. If you turn on a TV right now, you will get some sort of reception if you're tuned into a channel. Just like TV, your thoughts are pictures. Thoughts start as pictures in your mind but if you take action the thoughts become manifested in your reality field. Tune into a great channel and see what happens!

If you stop to think about your physical world right now and look at everything in your line of vision that was produced by man, everything you see in our world started as someone's thought. That is powerful! Almost everything is a solution to a condition that man, in his evolution, came across.

Consider the chair you're sitting in right now. I'm guessing that at a certain time in history someone got tired of moving boulders into caves to sit on. So a chair was invented. Someone thought about it first. How about the wheel? That started as an idea in someone's mind. Of course I can go on and on with millions, even billions of illustrations about thought but I will leave it there for now.

Some preach that thought alone can get you whatever you want. However, thought without action is useless. Action is the moving of ideas into reality. Reality becomes experience. Your thoughts are built on your previous experience, and experience is built on your previous thoughts. As you can see, your thoughts and your life are a circular pattern. If you want to change your life, you need to get different thoughts and beliefs in your mind. Your new thoughts will provide new experiences and then all of a sudden you realize a new happier life. One that you choose!

Choice

Your life today as you live it is a result of your thoughts about it. The Universe will always provide what you think about. So why not submerge yourself in thoughts about things you like and want? Submersion is key.

If you want to be a professional in anything, you can't just think about it all day and expect it to become manifest. If you want to be a doctor, you have to go to medical school. What medical school does is submerge you in having thoughts about the profession. In a certain amount of years you become a doctor in your reality. If you want to be a professional athlete, you must live the sport you chose every day, 24 hours a day. If you're not obsessed (in a good passionate way) you will never make it.

This type of submersion is called the "be, do, have" paradigm that Neale Donald Walsch explained in his book, *Conversations with God*.

You must act like the thing you want to **be**, and **do** the things it takes to be that and then you will **have** what your heart desires

Again, take the example of a doctor. You decide you want to be a doctor to help people or for the prestige or whatever your reasons are to have that designation. You must first proclaim your status, "I want to be a doctor." You will continue to "want" to be a doctor until you get accepted to medical school. Once accepted, you have to change your attitude and say, "I AM" becoming a doctor. And, now, you must do the things to get there. Now that you have decided to "be" a doctor and are "doing" the things to be a doctor, it is inevitable that you will become a doctor and have the things being a doctor will bring you. All you really did was decide and then take *action* by submerging yourself in the medical field.

Remember when you were a kid, elders always asked, "What do you want to BE when you grow up?" Once you grew up and got a job people ask you, "What do you DO for a living?"

There's a difference between being and doing. Being comes from the soul. No encumbrances, no reality, just pure choice. Doing is a worldly, ego-based notion. Most of the time what your body is doing is not your passion, it is *not* what your heart desires. You "do" a job but when you follow your passion, you are "being" what your soul is calling for your path.

EXERCISE: THE FUEL TO CHANGE

1. Write down a time when you did something, then asked yourself, "Why the heck did I do that?"

2. Now write down other choices that you could have made and the possible outcomes those choices would have brought.

3. Write down some of the things you know you are afraid of. Be honest with yourself. Flying, heights, water, etc.

4. Now, next to each of the fears you wrote down, write an "L" next to it if you *learned* that fear or an "E" if you had an actual *experience* that gave you that fear.

Do you see a pattern appearing?

5. Look at yourself in the mirror. What are the labels you use to describe yourself?

6. Now write down the new characteristics you want to describe you.

7. For five minutes, without stopping, write a description of what you want your life to look like. Add as much detail as possible. How does your new life feel, smell, taste?

3

A HISTORY LESSON

Before you go further, you need to take a bit of time to understand more about where fears come from and to evaluate the fears that are holding you back.

As I mentioned in the last chapter, fear is not something we are born with. Newborns react, when they are hungry, need a new diaper or are otherwise uncomfortable, by crying. Crying usually resolves the issue because Mom and Dad respond to the cries with action.

If a baby is exposed to a loud noise, they will startle. But, so do you and it's not because you are afraid, it is because you are startled by the loud noise, the reaction is innate – you're born with it. Human beings react to being startled in two unique ways, often called fight or flight.

In a flight response, the person who is startled will curl inward and move away from the perceived problem. They often bring their arms up across their body towards their mouth and they might scream or yelp.

Fight responders will do almost the complete opposite. They will typically move towards the problem, arms out, hands clenched, ready to break something or someone.

If you have a few minutes, go to YouTube and search for videos where the snowman scares people. Check out: https://www.youtube.com/watch?v=rgrr6b6Vt6M

People blissfully pass the docile looking over-sized snowman. But, the person inside has other plans. He repeatedly comes to life, startling everyone around him.

As you watch a few of these videos, you'll start to see flight groups and fight groups as they react to the snowman. Most interesting is when a couple is startled and one reacts with flight and the other fight.

So, if we aren't born with fears, where do they come from?

As children, we learn from two key inputs. The first input is the environment around us. When we first touch snow, we discover that snow is cold and wet. The same lessons are learned over and over as we explore our world.

Some inputs are extreme, such as touching a hot stove or sticking something in an electrical outlet (you did, right?). Each of the inputs enters our subconscious through our senses. We touch things, smell things, see and taste things. Each of these interactions has a significant impact on our subconscious minds, but the impact is not pure.

At any time in our childhood, something we like can become something we hate. We can also learn to not enjoy something we previously loved to eat. If a child loves pizza, that love might be diminished by a bad experience or experiences with pizza and they will likely become an adult who doesn't like pizza.

The opposite is also true. Many parents encourage children to try new foods and experiences. Sometimes, the experience creates a lifelong enjoyment. In others, the enjoyment follows a period where we did not enjoy a food as a child. Our palette has developed and refined, so the taste of foods has changed.

It is the same with experiences. As a child, I loved the crazy rides at the amusement park. But, as an adult, a roller coaster ride lasts far longer for me than for other riders because it takes a long time for my stomach to settle back down. I never had a bad experience with a ride as a child, but I have aged and my sense of balance has apparently changed.

Inputs are shaped by our genetic coding and life experiences. When children are teething, some parents use raw vegetables as a tool their child can use to chew on. These kids often age with a love of raw vegetables, while others won't touch a vegetable with a ten-foot pole. Why? The genetic code in each of us helps to interpret all of the inputs we are experiencing.

The one key to all of these inputs is that they start as a physical experience. Our senses explore and take in data at an amazing pace and our brain is chronically and meticulously cataloging all of this data into files for later use.

But, there is also a mental influence on our lives. This input comes from the people around us. As young children our parents, along with other loved ones, are primarily responsible for shaping us. How our parents view and interact with the world leaves a deep imprint on each of us.

Likewise, siblings are influencing us. There has been a lot of research surrounding birth order and how it shapes people, and there is universal agreement that the oldest child enters adolescence and adulthood differently than the youngest.

Other friends and family members will also shape us, to a lesser extent. But, the people that are shaping us do not stop at the people nearest us. The community at large, the television we watch, the music we listen to, the books we read, etc. all build the "me" that takes on the world.

So, can you guess what happens when your parent constantly reminds you to, "be careful" every time you leave the house? You'll probably learn to be careful, perhaps too careful.

The same influence can be seen in a child's experience with money. If a child constantly hears that "money is the root of all evil," it is highly likely that he/she will subconsciously avoid wealth as an adult. Likewise, if a person's childhood is spent in great poverty, this too will have a deep effect on them later in life. As a person gets older, gets a job and starts to make money, he or she will always go back to a set point that is financial comfortable for them. For instance, if someone grew up in a blue-collar working family and was invited to the founder of his company's house of a dinner party, he or she might feel uncomfortable or out of place in what might be a lavish setting. This is mainly because they may have been taught that people with money are bad people.

When I was a child, my father was a New York City Police Officer. He was the negative, suspicious type. I recall whenever I pointed out something like a cool, expensive car such as a Corvette or Jaguar my dad, without missing a beat would say, "Probably a drug dealer." Little did he know he was shaping my perspective of the *energy* called money. I later learned that my father had this drug dealer reaction, not because he was a cop, but because that is what his immigrant parents unknowingly taught him about people who are flashy with their money. He was just repeating what he was taught. …No hard feelings dad.

There's an old story of the pot roast. A young mother was cooking a pot roast that is a large hunk of meat. She cut off the edges of the pot roast before placing in the pot and seasoning it. Her young daughter, gleefully helping asked, "Mom, why did you cut the ends off of the meat?" The young mom explained, "It's an old family recipe. That's the way grandma taught me to cook it. Later that afternoon, the grandma came over to enjoy the family festivities and the traditional pot roast. The young, inquisitive granddaughter asked, "Grandma, why do you and mom cut the ends of the roast before you put it in the pot?" Grandma, without a blink, retorted, "When I was starting my family, we couldn't afford to buy another pot that was large enough for a roast so I used to cut the edges off to fit the meat in the pot."

Wow, how many things do we do or even just think that are of no use to us at all!

What connects our inputs and experiences is something I choose to call consequence. The hot stove input becomes "bad," because the burn on our hand hurts a lot. Likewise, a wonderfully healthy food that causes us to vomit more than once will probably be something we will steer away from.

My beautiful daughter, Andrea, loved chicken soup when she was a toddler. At one point she came down with the flu and my mother-in-law made Andrea an awesome pot of chicken soup, also known as Jewish penicillin. Andrea devoured it like it was her last meal. Suddenly she became queasy and exclaimed in her little, three-year old voice, "I'M GUNNA THROW!!!" She proceeded to regurgitate all that wonderful soup. Now, more than twenty years later, Andrea will not go near chicken soup even though it was one of her favorite foods as a kid.

Good and bad are being constantly shaped in our subconscious by the consequences of our data inputs and experiences.

So, our experiences and the influences of our loved ones mold us early in life. But, what about those "rebels" who move against everything they are taught? How do we explain them?

Well, remember fight or flight? Yes, some people rebel against everything they were taught. The results of this rebellion might be a good thing or a bad thing, but this person is simply "fighting" instead of just going with the flow of their influences and experiences.

As teenagers, many of us allow our friends and people outside our family to be greater influences on us than our parents. This is perfectly normal. We are asserting our partial independence and beginning to choose how WE define our lives. But, that definition is still being influenced by our early years, even if we want to deny it.

Whether we are labeled a "rebel" or just go with the flow, we enter adulthood as the sum of our experiences. Some we are clearly aware of, like the hot stove. Others, such as unhealthy obsessions or many addictions may have more vague origins. These may lie dormant in our subconscious for years or may become active earlier.

I need to stress something here. I am using the word "rebel" to help you understand the concept. BUT, as you will learn shortly, my opinion of your choices should not be anything more than another input in your decision-making process. The same should be true of your inputs from anyone else.

What if?

We are brought up and taught to take care because you don't know what fate has stored around the corner. Because of this we live with a sense of fear looming in the background. We take that fear to our everyday lives and decisions. There's always the "what if" quotient we have to deal with.

Wow, just think, what would you do if you knew you could not fail? Life would be very different, wouldn't it? In high school, would you have asked the prettiest girl or guy on a date? Would you apply for the position that had a responsibility of huge budgets and vast amounts of people? Would you have chosen a career that was more fulfilling and not just safe?

Take the Safe Route

Our teachers, preachers and parents have all told us to take the safe route. It's not their fault. They think it's because they love us and don't want to see us get hurt or lose. But, if you think about it, it's really about them. They do not want to have to deal with you losing and of course, the folks who tell you not to take the risk simply do not want you to succeed. Your success will remind them of their lack of drive. They actually may fear that they will have to get off the couch and do something otherwise you will get ahead of them in some way. Some people just want to have control. They will tell you that they know people who have tried things and failed or suffered. Others do not like change, even if it is a change in *your* life. They need to have you categorized and compartmentalized for their convenience.

Sometimes, people go to the wrong people for advice. As an example, if someone is making a business move they should consult an attorney and an accountant. However, those types of people are trained to be the devil's advocate and will point out every possible negative "what it" situation that can go wrong and can talk a person out of doing something great with a business. In addition, if you take this idea to its logical conclusion, if a lawyer gives advice to move ahead with a business deal because it sounds great to her, that attorney is open to negative repercussions if the deal fails. After all, the attorney said it was a good deal. You paid for that advice and guidance and now you lost a boatload of money. Might someone go after the attorney for damages? It's possible. Because of this scenario, it is very rare that a professional will give someone his or her blessing on something that has inherent risk associated with it.

When seeking advice we are rarely are told of the people who took a chance, who took a left turn, persisted and succeeded. To balance the scales, I took the liberty of assembling 26 notable people who had no special upbringing, faced adversity and forged ahead and succeeded despite all odds:

1. Henry Ford: While Ford is today known for his innovative assembly line and American-made cars, he wasn't an instant success. In fact, his early businesses failed and left him broke five times before he founded the successful Ford Motor Company.

2. R. H. Macy: Most people are familiar with this large department store chain, but Macy didn't always have it easy. Macy started and failed SEVEN businesses before finally hitting big with his store in New York City.

3. Soichiro Honda: The billion-dollar business that is Honda began with a series of failures and some interesting, fortunate turns of luck. Honda was turned down by Toyota Motor Corporation for a job after interviewing as an engineer, leaving him unemployed for quite some time. He started making scooters of his own at home, and spurred on by his neighbors, finally started his own business.

4. Harland David Sanders: Perhaps better known as Colonel Sanders of Kentucky Fried Chicken fame, Sanders had a hard time selling his chicken recipe at first. In fact, his famous secret chicken recipe was rejected 1,009 times before a restaurant accepted it.

5. Walt Disney: Today Disney rakes in billions from merchandise, movies and theme parks around the world, but Walt Disney himself had a bit of a rough start. A newspaper editor fired him because, he "lacked imagination" and had no good ideas." After that, Disney started a number of short-lived businesses and ended with bankruptcy and failure. He kept plugging along, however, and eventually found a recipe for success that worked.

6. Albert Einstein: Most of us take Einstein's name as synonymous with genius, but he didn't always show such promise. Einstein did not speak until he was four and did not read until he was seven, causing his teachers and parents to think he was mentally handicapped, slow and anti-social. Eventually, he was expelled from school and was refused admittance to the Zurich Polytechnic School. It might have taken him a bit longer, but most people would agree that he caught on pretty well in the end, winning the Nobel Prize and changing the face of modern physics.

7. Thomas Edison: In his early years, teachers told Edison he was "too stupid to learn anything." Work was no better, as he was fired from his first two jobs for not being productive enough. Even as an inventor, Edison made 1,000 unsuccessful attempts at inventing the light bulb. Of course, all those unsuccessful attempts finally resulted in the design that worked and changed the world.

8. Orville and Wilbur Wright: These brothers battled depression and family illness before starting the bicycle shop that would lead them to experimenting with flight. After numerous attempts at creating flying machines, several years of hard work, and tons of failed prototypes, the brothers finally created a craft that could get airborne and stay there.

9. Winston Churchill: This Nobel Prizewinning, twice-elected Prime Minster of the United Kingdom wasn't always as well regarded as he is today. Churchill struggled in school

and failed the sixth grade. After school, he faced many years of political failures, as he was defeated in every election for public office until he finally became the Prime Minister at the ripe old age of 62.

10. Abraham Lincoln: While today he is remembered as one of the greatest leaders of our nation, Lincoln's life wasn't so easy. In his youth he went to war a captain and returned a private (if you're not familiar with military ranks, just know that private is as low as it goes.) Lincoln didn't stop failing there, however. He was defeated many times before getting elected to public office.

11. Oprah Winfrey: Most people know Oprah as one of the most iconic faces on TV as well as one of the richest and most successful women in the world. Oprah faced a hard road to get to that position, however, enduring a rough and often abusive childhood as well as numerous career setbacks, including being fired from her job as a television reporter because she was "unfit for TV."

12. Jerry Seinfeld: Just about everybody knows who Seinfeld is, but the first time the young comedian walked on stage at a comedy club, he looked out at the audience, froze and was eventually jeered and booed off of the stage. Seinfeld knew he could do it, so he went back the next night, completed his set to laughter and applause, and the rest is history.

13. Fred Astaire: In his first screen test, the testing director of MGM noted that Astaire "Can't act. Can't sing. Slightly bald. Can dance a little." Astaire went on to become an incredibly successful actor, singer and dancer and kept that note in his Beverly Hills home to remind him of where he came from.

14. Charlie Chaplin: It's hard to imagine film without the iconic Charlie Chaplin, but his act was initially rejected by Hollywood studio chiefs because they felt it was a little too nonsensical to ever sell.

15. Lucille Ball: During her career, Ball had thirteen Emmy nominations and four wins, also earning the Lifetime Achievement Award from the Kennedy Center Honors. Before starring in I Love Lucy, Ball was widely regarded as a failed actress and a B movie star. Even her drama instructors didn't feel she could make it, telling her to try another profession. She, of course, proved them all wrong.

16. Vincent Van Gogh: During his lifetime, Van Gogh sold only one painting, and this was to a friend and only for a very small amount of money. While Van Gogh was never a success during his life, he continued to paint, sometimes starving to complete his over 800 known works. Today, they bring in hundreds of millions, which sucks for Vincent or Vinnie, as his best friends used to call him.

17. Theodor Seuss Giesel: Today nearly every child has read The Cat in the Hat or Green Eggs and Ham. Yet 27 different publishers rejected Dr. Seuss's first book, *To Think That I Saw It on Mulberry Street.*

18. Charles Schultz: Schultz's Peanuts comic strip has had enduring fame, yet this cartoonist had every cartoon he submitted rejected by his high school yearbook staff. Even after high school, Schultz didn't have it easy, rejected for a position working with Walt Disney – who should have known better after what he'd been through.

19. Steven Spielberg: While today Spielberg's name is synonymous with big budget, he was rejected from the University of Southern California School of Theater, Film and Television three times. He eventually attended school at another location, only to drop out to become a director before finishing. Thirty-five years after starting his degree, Spielberg returned to school in 2002 to finally complete his work and earn his BA.

20. J. K. Rowling: Rowling may be rolling in a lot of Harry Potter dough today, but before she published the series of novels, she was nearly penniless, severely depressed, divorced, trying to raise a child on her own while attending school and writing a novel. Rowling went from depending on welfare to survive to being one of the richest women in the world in a span of only five years through her hard work and determination.

21. Wolfgang Amadeus Mozart: Mozart began composing at the age of five, writing over 600 pieces of music that today are lauded as some of the best ever created. Yet during his lifetime, Mozart didn't have such an easy time, and he was often restless, leading to his dismissal from a position as a court musician in Salzburg. He struggled to keep the support of the aristocracy and died with little to his name.

22. Elvis Presley: As one of the best-selling artists of all time, Elvis has become a household name even years after his death. But back in 1954, Elvis was still a nobody, and Jimmy Denny, manager of the Grand Ole Opry, fired Elvis Presley after just one performance telling him, "You ain't going nowhere, son. You ought to go back to driving a truck."

23. The Beatles: Few people can deny the lasting power of this super group, still popular with listeners around the world today. Yet when they were just starting out, a recording company told them no. They were told, "we don't like their sound, and guitar music is on the way out," two things the rest of the world couldn't have disagreed with more.

24. Ludwig van Beethoven: In his formative years, young Beethoven was incredibly awkward on the violin and was often so busy working on his own compositions that he neglected to practice. Despite his love of composing, his teachers felt he was hopeless at it and would never succeed with the violin or in composing. Beethoven kept plugging along, however, and

composed some of the best-loved symphonies of all time–five of them while he was completely deaf.

25. Michael Jordan: Most people wouldn't believe that a man often lauded as the best basketball player of all time was actually cut from his high school basketball team. Luckily, Jordan didn't let this setback stop him from playing the game and he has stated, "I have missed more than 9,000 shots in my career. I have lost almost 300 games. On 26 occasions I have been entrusted to take the game winning shot, and I missed. I have failed over and over and over again in my life. And that is why I succeed."

26. Babe Ruth: You probably know Babe Ruth because of his home run record (714 during his career), but along with all those home runs came a pretty hefty amount of strikeouts as well (1,330 in all). In fact, for decades, he held the record for strikeouts. When asked about this he simply said, "Every strike brings me closer to the next home run."

The clear message here is: don't listen to your critics.

One I Personally Experienced

My wife Gina is retired from the New York City Police Department. She spent 20 years helping the people of New York. The NYPD has a great retirement and pension program. Upon completion of 20 years of service, any member may retire and immediately collect a pension regardless of their age.

Gina, preparing for retirement or actually the next phase of her life, opened a business two years before retirement that was being managed by our niece. In addition to opening a business and as part of a mid-life – I want to do something I've never done before and confront my fears thought process;

Gina took a stand-up comedy class. Lo and behold, Gina was a natural at stand-up comedy. She proceeded to take more classes and honed her comedy and acting skills.

As an interesting turn of events that were out of our control, the economy slowed down and other trials within Gina's business took place, including a loss of passion for the business and we had to close down Gina's business almost exactly one year after she fully retired from the NYPD.

As part of civil service law in New York City, a retired NYPD officer is permitted to return to their position and salary within 365 days of retirement. In May of 2008 we realized that Gina business would take a toll equal to almost our entire life savings. Gina had to decide at that point to either go back to the job or follow her dreams and what seemed to be her natural calling in comedy and acting.

We sat at the kitchen table in July 2008, poured over our bills and debt, being interrupted by collection agency phone calls, trying to decide by July 27, if she was going back to being a cop or not.

We left the table with the decision that she would not forfeit her dreams and happiness for the sake of money. Four days later, on August 1, Gina received a phone call from a national comedy troupe called the Italian Chicks. The founder and organizer of the Troupe, Maryann Misano, heard about Gina's recent success on the Long Island Comedy circuit and asked Gina to join their troupe and be the mistress of ceremonies at all of their gigs! www.TheItalianChicks.com.

I'd say that was a confirmation from the Universe! This told us that Gina made the right choice and was on the right path. Many great things have happened in Gina's career since being involved with the Italian Chicks including being featured on TV shows such as *Today with Kathy Lee and Hoda* and *World*

News Tonight with Diane Sawyer, plus numerous magazine articles and books all telling the story of Gina's transformation. She is on a direct path to realizing her dreams.

The lesson I learned by Gina's going from Cop to Comedian is: when you tempt fate, slumbering forces within you and outside of you come to your assistance and guide you to where you need to go. Someone who has not stared fear in the face and made a choice for his or her soul cannot understand this notion.

As Babe Ruth Said: "Never let the fear of striking out get in your way."

Does Religion Hold Us Back?

The Media, newspapers, TV, radio and now websites and blogs, use fear tactics to build ratings and sell more advertising. It's in the media's best interest to breed fear. Unfortunately, what we fear most is what we attract. Every time you buy a newspaper or tune into a news show you are voting for more of the same.

Organized religion has a strong interest in controlling us too. We have to believe that bad things are going to happen to us if we don't follow the rules. Ultimately we will end up in hell if we don't listen to the preachers.

At the risk of sounding blasphemous, I believe in God, but I do not believe that he wants to hurt us or subject us to damnation if we do not obey "the rules."

If you subscribe to the Christian-Jewish philosophy, you know that God created humans in the likeness of Him. You also believe that God is perfect in every way. Hence if we are created by God to be like God then we are perfect. So, no need to worry there.

We are on this planet to experience life as God would, as people such as Jesus, Buddha, Krishna, Ja and all the masters did. We all have the ability to live like masters, in perfect harmony with God, nature and the Universe. Problem is we have been told since we are born that we are not perfect. We have lessons to learn. We are born into sin. I revert back to the above paragraph. We were created by God to be like God so we are perfect. So no need to fear.

Every religion or philosophy known to man is based in the ideology of there is nothing to fear, just live by the golden rule: do onto others as you would have done onto you. Have compassion for your fellow brother and sister. I heard somewhere that in the modern King James Version of the Bible it says, "do not fear" 365 times. One for each day of the year. (I have never actually counted the phrase in the Bible myself).

Now, if we believe that we are like God and have powers like masters who have walked the earth in the past, we can live freely and follow our dreams. We don't have to worry about if we can make it.

Do animals and birds in the forest worry about where their food is going to come from? Is grass concerned with where water will come from? Why would we, God's most prized possession, be concerned about what we need to live?

Most of the time, what gets in our way is our ego. We are too concerned about what people think of us. We need to keep up appearances. We need to have the car and the body the media says we should have. This is where our dissatisfaction with life comes from.

We have become a culture that is hooked on MORE. We need more of everything! This is the way we compare ourselves against our neighbors. If we lived naturally and were not concerned with possessions we would have no stress. With all of your stuff you need insurance and locks and safes and alarm systems. You cannot face the thought of losing anything. I think it's stated perfectly in Chuck Palahniuk's book and movie, *The Fight Club* when the character Tyler Durden says, "You can't have anything until you've lost everything."

The more you have the more you're jailed by your stuff. By now, you should be saying to yourself, "sure I want to follow my dreams but how will I pay my mortgage? How can I make my car payments and send the kids to private school?"

Exactly, we have bought into the system and now the system controls our lives. We become our possessions and not who we really are. You become your title at work and who your family and friends think you are and should be.

This is where the ownership of your stuff becomes your warden. You cannot fathom not having your stuff. How will you be able to show your face? What will your friends and family think about you? This is why we approach our life from the perspective of protecting ourselves from loss. We put risk away and live a life that is perceived to be safe, or at least controlled to the best of our ability.

We are born into this world with nothing. We will leave with nothing. Have you ever seen an armored truck in a funeral procession? Death, as you know, is life's only guarantee. We do we spend our very short time on earth trying to accumulate and keep our stuff safe. It seems like a pointless waste of time in the big picture.

Life is temporary and temporal. Our lives are a fleeting moment in time. Don't take yourself so seriously. None of us are that important. The world functioned before we got here and it will do just fine after we leave.

I have always tried to have that big picture mindset, especially when I am confronted with a stressful situation. In 2000 when I was working for the Long Island Rail Road, I was in charge of the print shop and poster and sign production. 2000 was also the year of the first baseball World Series subway series between the New York Mets and Yankees.

The whole city was jubilant and frankly in an excited uproar. Apparently, my bosses were taken up in this excitement also. Once we found out the dates of the World Series and times the teams would play at the old Shea Stadium, which the Long Island Rail Road serviced directly, I was ordered to drop everything and start production of signs for this historic baseball and New York City event.

I reminded my bosses, as I refused to "drop everything," that the last time I checked, Shea Stadium has not added any additional seating. Since Shea Stadium was built in 1964, the Long Island Rail Road has been servicing it without issue since it opened. The Long Island Rail Road has a special operating plan that calls for extra trains and personal to shepherd the throngs of fans to the events at the stadium. We have serviced this station for 36 years without issue. Why is this event any different from any sold out game aside from all the hoopla?

The point of the story is: everything is what you make it. If you choose to get caught up in a media frenzy you will cause yourself undue stress. Why not put all circumstances and situations in the "big picture" perspective. Nothing is that important. All things pass. Time heals all wounds.

EXERCISE: FUEL TO CHANGE

Using the list of fears you created after the last chapter, look back into your past and consider what experiences shaped those fears and write them down next to each fear.

Make a list of things your parents repeated to you most often. What did they say about love, money, etc.? Add a secondary list for other loved ones you spent childhood time with.

Are there any physical experiences you remember from your childhood that you might consider negative? What happened right after the incident (did you get right back on that horse after you fell off?)? Did people around you encourage you to try again? Did you? Why or why not? Were you more successful the second time?

For me, a life-changing incident happened to me in 7th grade when I asked out my first girl. I knew from her friends that she liked me. It was in the bag – a done deal. After weeks of practicing in the mirror, I finally asked her to be my steady girl. She abruptly said no! Her friends were watching and I was crushed. Actually, it was probably more embarrassed than anything else. After years of therapy I realized that I have never asked out another girl on a date in my entire life since that seemingly innocent incident. In addition, I never spoke up at meetings or in a store when I was given the wrong change or in any other life situation. Everyone that I dated had to make it clear that they wanted to date me before I would engage. Even my wife of 25-years asked me out on our first date in 1983 in the hallways of Kingsborough community college in Brooklyn, NY. Little did that young 7th grade girl know what an impact she would make on the next 30 years of my life. However, I am grateful for her and that experience. If not for her and the introspection I went through I probably wouldn't be writing this book today.

4

BRING ON THE FEAR

Along our early journey as humans, we begin to develop fears. Whether or not they are appropriate or not is immaterial. To our subconscious, every fear we have is perfectly acceptable. Our fears either grow or shrink as we age.

Infants are only aware of the person they can see, smell or touch. Infants have no sense of loss when it comes to people. If you leave an infant with a babysitter, assuming that he or she responds to your baby's cues in much the same way you do, your infant will blissfully eat, sleep, poop and play.

But, as toddlers, children do notice the absence. Depending on their level of personal comfort, each child will react to leaving their parents differently, but typically they will not be happy about it. However, as the child learns that Mom and Dad really do come back just like they said they would, the anxiety diminishes or disappears completely. By our teenage years, we are BEGGING Mom and Dad to leave us alone.

Fear, simply defined, is a mechanism developed by our subconscious to protect us. Some fears are shaped by our actual experiences and some by our perception of the consequences. Most people would love to have a bank's money, but they don't rob the bank because the thought of being caught and imprisoned does not sound like a good time. This is an example of a healthy fear.

Some fears, however, are not healthy. Most deep phobias are not healthy, because they debilitate the person to a point where they can't function normally. Phobias are an extreme example of fears that are beyond healthy.

Many people dictate their lives by fears they aren't even aware of. I'm guessing you suspect you are one of these people because you are reading my book. Something inside you is telling you that there is a program in your subconscious that is holding you back.

The manifestations of fears are as broad as the fears themselves. Someone who was thin as a child may become obese because their subconscious has decided that obesity will protect them from another heartbreak similar to one they have already experienced.

Likewise, a person who is silently terrified of being poor may stay in a horrible job that they hate, working with people who mistreat them and being undercompensated for their efforts only so that they can avoid their perception of the consequences of poverty.

Does this sound crazy to you? I'll bet you a steak dinner that you know someone who is living his or her life or some part of his or her life driven only by a subconscious fear. It might even be you. You might know someone who talks about wishing they could fall in love, lamenting that it won't happen because they are overweight. Yet, every diet they try fails. Confused? Let's add some glue to the conversation and I think you'll see how this all comes together.

EXERCISE: FUEL TO CHANGE

Make a list of friends or family members that appear to be operating some portion of their life due to fear. Consider that fear can drive positive or negative actions. Typically people who overcompensate in one area of their life are fearful of the opposite coming to light. For instance, a workaholic is sometimes a person who is terrified to be poor.

5

ADDING SOME GLUE

Let's add some glue to everything you have read so far. Your subconscious is chronically being bombarded by data and experiences, including sensory inputs and the influence of the people we come in contact with.

Then, our subconscious dictates policy to our conscious mind and we live our lives accordingly. If our subconscious is convinced that money is a bad thing, our conscious doesn't tell our subconscious that this isn't correct. Our conscious simply walks through life simply following instructions.

That overweight friend who can't find love and can't lose weight? Somewhere along the way, your friend's subconscious decided that extra pounds were needed as a protection.

The reason that the diets fail is that most diets focus on the conscious mind. The diet program tells them that they can do it, but their subconscious won't let it happen. Or, worse yet, they will lose weight and then they will gain it back again because their subconscious is bringing them back into "balance."

At the other extreme is that friend you might have that is constantly jumping from one relationship to another. This friend has "learned" to only enjoy the honeymoon period of relationships or is absolutely "convinced" that they are less of a person if they aren't in a relationship.

In fairness to most fears, society doesn't help. As a nation, we value physical beauty over internal beauty. We prefer fitness to flab. We celebrate celebrities with little or no talent. And, even though we hold wealthy people in high regard, we also don't encourage entrepreneurship and business risk-taking. Steve Jobs, Howard Schultz and Richard Branson are the exceptions, not the rule.

I suggest the media is a big negative influence in our personal development. I recommend going on a media diet. Cancel your subscription to the news. Turn off the TV. See how your outlook on life changes. Many of you will say, wait, I need to know what's going on in the world! How will I know? I say you don't need to know what's going on in your town or across the globe. Take a minute to stop and reflect on the news that you read or heard today. Does it directly affect you right now? Can you change it or affect it today? I bet not. Let it go and focus on what you can change. The one thing you can work on today is YOU!

Most people I know start out every day with a cup of coffee and a newspaper. They don't realize it, but they are meditating or praying for bad news to start their day. No wonder your coworker is in a bad mood. After reading about the murders, fires and stock market slide, I would be depressed too! Imagine starting the day with positive info like a book by a motivational speaker. There are literally thousands to choose from.

In summary, our fears are created and supported in our subconscious mind in a desire to protect us. Some fears are normal and healthy, but others are not.

So, armed with this understanding of how you got to be who you are, it's time to start doing something about it.

EXERCISE: FUEL TO CHANGE

Make a short list of examples of how media and other inputs use fear to convince you or sell you something OR create a false outcome to lure you. Does that new car really attract supermodels?

Write down an example of some part of your life where you have repeatedly failed. Is it weight loss, relationships, getting promoted at work or something else? Under the example, look inside yourself and consider how your past might be influencing the outcome.

6

GOOD FEAR, BAD FEAR

Although I generally try to not label fears as good or bad, there are some fears that should probably be considered good ones. For example, the strong desire to run from an enraged wild animal is generally going to be a good fear. However, it is better to lie down and play dead when confronted with an angry bear, according to the experts. (Advice I hope to never have to put to the test). But, the fear itself is appropriate.

Some fears are innate, like this fear of an angry animal with lots of teeth. But, most fears are not innate and none are programmed during fetal development. Fears are also not instinctual. Fear, like many things in your conscious and subconscious mind, is learned. Fears are molded by experience.

But, unless you are living close to life's edge on a regular basis, the vast majority of the circumstances or outcomes that you may fear will NEVER come true!!! Repeat that last sentence to yourself a few times.

You might fear financial disaster or distress, yet never experience it, even if you take some financial risks. Fear of heartbreak, often the result of a past breakup, won't increase or decrease the odds of another broken heart.

But, in each of these examples, fear can be softened or eliminated by thought, education and/or experience. A good relationship, even if it ends, can teach you to be less fearful of that broken heart and small financial "risks" can open you up to endless possibilities, including owning your own business.

The key to fear is how it is managed versus how much it manages YOU.

Mark Twain noted that one never overcomes fear. He said that courage is the resistance to fear, mastery of fear – not absence of fear.

Live Naturally

There was no effort to conceive you. Your parents made love, that's what creates life.

Without any effort you grow from a seed to a 6-pound baby in nine months. Your mother just had to exist for this to happen. She did not have to apply any skills. My mother even smoked when she was pregnant with me. (I realized that's why I'm short. That is my story and I'm sticking to it.)

After you were born, at about one-year old you started to learn how to live un-naturally. Your parents started to interfere with your mental development and you've been fighting it ever since.

Take a look around and count how many things happen without effort. The sun rises and warms the earth, trees grow and perform photosynthesis. Waves crash on the beach. Why do we humans choose to not live naturally?

Well, we are taught by parents and organized religions that we are not good enough and need to worry about loss, to mention one notion. Our parent's first words to us are "Be Careful!" I don't blame them for this; it's all they knew. They were probably concerned about you taking your first steps and falling.

What would have happened if they weren't there to instruct you how to walk? You would have just walked! You would have figured it out.

You would have wobbled a bit, fell and got back up and tried again. You didn't need an instructor to tell you to get back up a try again.

This "be careful" and take care attitude unfortunately carried into every facet of our lives. Why do we stave off death – it's the only guarantee of life. Imagine if we embraced death, looked at it straight in the eye and moved forward with our life anyway.

If we decided to live life naturally and embrace the experience from a state of love instead of fear we would have no worries.

EXERCISE: FUEL TO CHANGE

Take a look at your list of fears and write down small steps you might want to take to overcome the fear. If you are afraid of heights, this might mean taking a trip each week to progressively higher and higher floors of a famous building and journaling how the view changes at each level. If you are afraid to leave your job and strike out on your own, it might mean spending two hours every weekend researching possible business ideas. Are you afraid to love? Start looking inside yourself. Perhaps it actually has to do with a fear of loss and suffering. There are many, many great books to start reading on this subject if fear of loss is the case.

Implement the smallest step on your list. Do that step over and over until you no longer have any kind of negative reaction to the step. This will be your marker to add another step.

Make a schedule for when you will add additional steps to eliminate or minimize your fear. You should define the pace of your schedule, but try to be a little bit aggressive about the process.

7

MANIFESTING AND
THE LAW OF ATTRACTION

I was having a conversation with a friend the other day about manifesting. I was explaining to her, and to you, that anyone could manifest anything they wanted. They could manifest wealth, love, peace and physical health. My friend had grown up in a very difficult environment. Her mother had mental health issues and both parents were drug addicts. Out of respect for my friend, I'll leave the rest of the details out, but I can tell you that the details I just outlined were the GOOD news in her childhood.

So, she was genuinely interested in her own ability to shape her future into what she wanted as opposed to accepting her "lot in life." She asked me how many people actually knew they had this power. I told her it was less than one percent of the population. She then asked me a good question. What happens to everyone else?

Manifesting sounds a bit new age to many people. But, it is actually very simple and only has three components.

First, you decide what you want some part of your life to look like. Let's use your job and income as an example. Let's say that you want to be your own boss and have notable financial freedom. No problem. Close your eyes and imagine what that life looks like. The more details you can insert into your vision, the better. What is your life like when you wake up in the morning? Do you have a cup of coffee from your custom-built cappuccino machine? What does your home look like?

As you add details, take a moment to consider why certain details are important. For example, if you grew up in a home where the power was frequently shut off due to the bill not being paid, your vision might include lots of lights and constantly flowing hot water. There's no right or wrong because this is your vision.

Try to include lots of sensory detail as well. Imagine what you are eating and how it tastes and smells. When you engage your senses and get them in on the game, what you're trying to manifest gets put in the express lane. Sometimes this isn't easy. How am I supposed to know it feels like to drive that car or wear that suit? GO TAKE A TEST DRIVE! At least go to the dealership and sit in it. Smell the leather, touch it and see your hand on the gearshift. Make it real for you! Go and try on a designer suit or whatever it is for you.

No one wants "money" if it's not for certain things. Figure out what those things are for you and experience them. Remember the sensations of sight, smell, touch, sound or taste for that matter. (Don't lick the steering wheel – that would just be gross but you don't need millions to taste caviar. Consider how your new wardrobe feels against your skin. Pretty nice, right?

Write down your vision in a journal complete with all of your sensory perceptions. Some people also cut out pictures of things that represent their new life and glue them to a poster board, placing the board where they can often see it EVERYDAY.

The second step is to take action. I'm not suggesting you quit your current job, yet. Like any project, there are many little baby steps you can take. Start by taking a good hard look at how you spend money and what you spend it on. I have yet to meet anyone who couldn't save money if they put some work into it. Do you use coupons? Do you eat out more than you should? But, some of these baby steps can also be a lot of fun.

Action steps are important because manifesting is not a lottery. There is not a single thing in life worth having that does not require action and work.

The final step combines understanding the laws of the universe, expressing gratitude for what you already have and throwing away your clocks – in other words, stop putting time limitations on your manifesting.

The world we live in has infinite everything. There is more than enough money, more than enough love, more than enough everything all around you. Once you understand this, it becomes much easier to understand how anything you want can come to you. You lose the fears of loss and failure.

Gratitude is often the hardest part to master. How do you become thankful for something you don't think you have yet? Well, you just do. My mentors say, "Act as if." Act as if you have the money, the car, the relationship, etc. Close your eyes again and tell yourself how grateful you are that every one of your desires is already fulfilled, as if it has arrived. You will be surprised how peaceful you will become as you learn to be grateful for everything.

Have you ever gone out of your way to help someone and not even receive a "thank you" in return? Or, do you have a relative or friend that calls only when they want something? (We all have one of these in our lives.) Do you want to pick up the phone when you see their number pop up on the caller ID of do you just want to hit the ignore button? Well the universe or God works the same way. If we only ask and ask again and never give gratitude the universe will push the ignore button on you!

Here's a funny story as an example. I have a friend, Jerry, who is amazing at manifesting. He has a wonderful life, income and family. He is also religious, so his gratitude is aimed at God. But, as good as he is at manifesting, he is a gratitude genius. The other day I was helping him to build a new deck. Every time something happened that you and I would see as bad, he said, "Thank you, God." He hit his finger with a hammer, hard, and said, "Thank you, God." Now that's gratitude!

But, life is life. Some days it may be really, really difficult to be grateful if you are not Jerry. How do you find gratitude when you are not really seeing anything to feel grateful for? Fake it. Sort of. Gratitude, especially when connected to manifesting, will often require you to be grateful for things you can't see. In fact, your ability to be excited and grateful for things to come is the essence of manifesting because you must live your life as if your desires are already in motion. Jesus always gave thanks and gratitude to His Father God before performing a miracle. He knew that his work would be manifested. Gratitude and faith are the keys to creating and manifesting on this earth.

In my experience, the tricky part comes with throwing away your clocks. I don't mean that you should physically throw away all of the clocks in your home. What I want you to understand is that the world around you has no concept of time. Mountains don't and neither do trees. We interpret tree rings and other physical findings relative to time, but the tree doesn't care. Time is manmade and if you think about it, time is just a way of keeping track of the changes in our life and nothing more.

Here's where things get touchy. The Universe will often give you exactly what you want, but not necessarily in the timeframe you gave it. But don't fret, the universe is never late. My mom always says, "God is seldom early but He is never late."

We live in a world of instant gratification. When we need information we just pick up the phone and ask SIRI for the answer. 9 out of 10 times we get what we ask for. But sometimes SIRI does not understand the question. Instead of giving up in getting the info you want just rephrase the question. If that doesn't work you may have to take some action and Google it yourself. But do you doubt for a minute that what you are asking for is impossible? NO!!! You know the answer is out there somewhere on the Internet. That is how the universe works. Sometimes you ask and dot see what you want immediately, rephrase your question. If that doesn't work dig a little deeper and be more specific, get more info. The universe will deliver to you exactly what you want.

Personally, I have a BHAG of owning a private jet. BHAG = Big Hairy Audacious Goal. I have a picture of a Lear Jet 55 on my vision board in my office. I've had it on my wall for five or so years. Recently, I became friends with a guy Nik who is a pilot. Taking flight lessons has been on my bucket list for 20 years, but I have always put it off. I asked Nik if he could teach me how to fly. He said, "Sure, just give me a call." The week after I originally met Nik I called his office. I asked him when we could start flight training? He said that he does not do flight training personally, but he'd hook me up with the best trainer on Long Island. Ok, that is good, I thought to myself but I'm confused. What do you do at the aviation, I asked him? Nik responded, "I'm the President and CEO." Awesome, I thought! He invited me to the airport for a tour. When we met he was excited to show me the offices and the school then we ventured out to the Hanger. He opened the door leading from his office to the humongous, brightly lit hanger and sitting right there before us was Nik's Lear 55. The exact plane I have on my wall in my office! I had to catch my breath as tears welled up in my eyes. Now, I still do not own the Lear Jet but I definitely brought it into my reality. I believe the Universe delivered!

If being your own boss is your heart's desire, then your action steps should include slashing your spending and increasing your savings. At the same time, you should also be educating yourself on everything related to entrepreneurship. There would be no point to the Universe giving you the opportunity to own a business if you knew little or nothing about business fundamentals? Again, you have to be a business owner in your mind before you own a business in reality.

At the same time, you must maintain that "attitude of gratitude," because there are so many gears turning to deliver your desire and you simply cannot see them all. As an example, consider a married couple. Can you imagine the millions of little steps, including choices each partner made, that their parents made, the weather, when they got the flu as a child, etc. that had to be part of a perfect machine in order for those two people to even meet? You can make yourself dizzy trying to think it through!! You need to imagine that same perfect machine working on your behalf no matter what you're trying to bring into existence.

Keep in mind; you can't CONTROL most of those gears. So, you might as well get grateful, get comfortable and focus on the action and thought items that are directly within your control. Anything else will not only make you crazy or depressed, but it will probably feed your fears. Once you make your request to the Universe, just let it go and the Universe will make it happen.

Manifesting also goes hand in hand with another principle commonly known as the Law of Attraction. Have you ever wondered why a bad thing happens to a good person? Blame the Law of Attraction. This law states that you attract everything that happens to you, good and bad.

Before we look at the Law of Attraction, I want to make sure you are clear on one final thought related to manifesting. You CANNOT manifest for other people. As much as you might wish, your ability to manifest is limited to you and your life. Others, knowingly or not, will manifest their own situations. So, you can manifest a wonderful and healthy relationship, but you will fail if you try to manifest on behalf of that "perfect" someone.

The Universe knows what is best for you. If you focus on a great relationship, the Universe will give you one at exactly the right time, assuming that you continue to work on other parts of your life while you are waiting and are grateful for the relationship as if you are already in it.

Sometimes, the connection is not easy to uncover. If Joe is a wonderful, loving person with lots of friends and a great life, why does Joe have a car accident? It might be because Joe was speeding or driving while distracted. But, even when the cause is obvious, the underlying cause is that Joe ATTRACTED the accident from his subconscious. Perhaps he was overly fearful of car accidents. Or, perhaps he was recently pondering why his life was so good and he never had any problems instead of focusing on gratitude. This is a huge point to understand. Nothing is random in this Universe. Everything happens because of someone's or many people's thoughts about it. Even if a particular victim is God-fearing, perfect in every way and gets run over by a bus, for some reason, some way, he manifested that bus running him over. This notion is extremely difficult to accept and process by most people, but if you can understand it and start taking responsibility for your thoughts your life will change dramatically.

I suggest thinking about your thoughts as currency. How would you spend your thoughts? If you accept that your thoughts have a direct effect on your life I bet you would not spend your thoughts irresponsibly.

The Law of Attraction is sometimes tough to grasp, because many people don't want to accept responsibility for what happens in their life. The woman who successfully sued McDonalds after being burned by the hot cup of coffee she was holding did not seem particularly concerned with her own responsibility. Is it not highly likely that putting a steaming cup of coffee between your legs in a moving vehicle might end with a bad outcome? Yet, the courts awarded her, and many others with frivolous lawsuits, millions of dollars cementing the idea in our society's collective brain that someone else is always to blame for our misfortunes. This is JUST NOT TRUE!

EVERYTHING that happens to you comes from your powerful ability to attract it. So, if you focus on your fears, what do you suppose is going to come into your life? Probably the very things you fear!!! But, if you focus on manifesting the opposite of those same fears, what do you now think will happen? You're right, the opposite!!!

If you ever wondered why some people seem to just have everything good fall into their laps, you are pondering the Law of Attraction. I'll bet you all the tea in China that this person, knowingly or not, isn't the least bit surprised at all the good. In fact, I'll bet the "EXPECT IT" factor is a normal part of who they are.

So, the answer to my friend's question about manifesting was simple. Everyone is attracting exactly what he or she wants, even if they don't realize that they are doing it!!! This is not the same as "getting what you deserve." But, if you want to answer why good things happen to bad people and vice versa, you are now in the loop.

This Law of Attraction thing is nothing new. You can read about it many great, timeless self-help and motivational books. Perhaps it's a coincidence, but I think not, most of these great books have the word THINK in their title: *Think and Grow Rich* by Napoleon Hill, *The Power of Positive Thinking* by Dr. Norman Vincent Peale, *The Magic of Thinking Big* by David Schwartz, *Everyday Positive Thinking* by Louise Hay and *Change your Thoughts, Change your Life* by Dr. Wayne Dyer, just to name a few. These are all excellent reads and I highly recommend them as you further your study into the power of your mind.

EXERCISE: FUEL TO CHANGE

Find a quiet place and close your eyes. Imagine the perfect life for you, in deep detail. How is each part of your new life perfect? Enjoy yourself as you tour your new life. Then, write down all that you remember from your journey.

Create a mantra or meditation for yourself. Write it down and place copies on your bathroom mirror, in your car, etc. Your mantra might be something, such as "I am so grateful for the amazing life I am living and how the best parts continue to manifest around me. Today, whether I see them or not, I am excited about all the machinery operating around me to continue to give me the extraordinary life I live."

8

WHERE DID MY DREAM GO?

Consistency is the last refuge of the unimaginative.

–Oscar Wilde

People start out in life with passion and enthusiasm. They hit a few roadblocks, hear a few no's and choose the status quo. Somewhere around age 40 people tend to have a "crisis" and realize they aren't happy.

Unhappiness turns into resentment. Resentment often turns into sickness. Once sickness manifests in the body, it's usually too late to turn things around and folks die in a sad state with tons of regret.

We are told to go to school, get a job and life will be good. How many people do you know who wake with enthusiasm and can't wait to get to a job? If you want to do your kids a favor, take their college tuition and invest it in real estate. Help them discover their heart's desires. They will be happier and more successful following their soul than getting a degree in something they have no passion about.

Unfortunately, colleges don't offer degrees in the laws of the universe the thing you need most to understand how to succeed. So instead of books on the history of calculus, give them the books listed in the back of this book. If their heart's desire is to be a doctor or some other profession where school is necessary then have at it. But so many kids today go to these schools that cost hundreds of thousands of dollars to study things like art, drama and anthropology leaving school with loans that will take YEARS to pay back only to get a job at their local department store for a little over minimum wage. Learn what you need to learn. Yes the world needs college graduates, but define what you "want" first and look at the whole picture.

Imagine doing something that you love for 20 or 30 years and living life to the fullest. If you did, you would probably live a lot longer and with fewer sick days taken. Just imagine the impact.

Look, we can all agree that we have a limited amount of time on this planet, why spend 80% of it looking forward to enjoying 20% at the end. Begin with the end in mind.

What's your vision, what steps can you take now to start a life that you'll love, one you can write a book about, one that Hollywood would make into a movie?

The first thing that comes to mind is: I need money. If you go through life with the notion I "need" money, you will continue to "need" money. You have to act like you have it and it will come. It is the Law of Attraction. Let me give you another example in simple terms:

It all starts with faith and confidence. You have to know that you know everything will work out great, like Jesus did. You can't approach life or any situation from any other angle.

Sometimes we feel that the odds are stacked against us. Again, if you believe that, then it will be the case. The fact of all matters is that the facts don't matter, only the truth matters. And the truth is simply what you believe in your heart.

Things are not always what they appear to be. For example, take a look outside. The world is obviously flat. If you didn't know better, you'd bet everything you have on someone trying to disprove that fact. It seems pretty clear to me.

It seems that the objects we see in our world are solid. Bang on the table nearest you. Seems pretty solid, doesn't it? If you used a high-powered microscope to inspect the wood or metal or glass, you'd learn that deep down at the Planck scale or sub-atom level, there are particles that are moving to create what seems like a solid. Everything is energy and everything is vibrating. The frequency something is vibrating is what makes it look and feel the way it does. There's mysterious scientific evidence that says; what we think we're dealing with in our world is not what it is. This is why I say that what we think are scientific facts are not facts at all. We are at a dawn of a new science that is at a scale so small we, as humans, can barely observe it. Moreover, quantum scientists are finding that depending who looks at something and when it is looked at – can change moment to moment. This information is changing how science is moving forward right now.

And, your thoughts are also energies that vibrate at certain levels. Through these vibrations you can actually *change* your reality. When a new life circumstance comes your way, there's no reason to resist it. How you perceive any situation is how you'll experience it. And that's all life is, just one experience after another. The secret is to be conscious enough to choose the experience you want and not just stand by and let experiences and situations chose you.

9

BUT, I'M AFRAID?

But, what about those fears that you have? Well, they're still there. In fact, as you become more aware of yourself, you'll probably notice them popping up more and more as you manifest your future. Either you'll hear a little voice telling you money is bad or you don't deserve it as you dream of a different financial life. Or, you'll notice that you have trouble staying focused on your manifestation. These are both good markers to your own fears.

Because fears are driven by your well-meaning subconscious, they are always based on good intentions. But, if a fear is holding you back, it is time for you to have a stern conversation with yourself.

Take some time and consider your fear. Don't just accept it at face value. Go deep. Why are you REALLY afraid to be self-employed? Is it a masked fear of poverty? Or, is it something else? Could it be that you don't trust yourself to be a disciplined boss to yourself? Do you feel that you don't deserve success and freedom?

Write down all of the possible sources for your fear. Consider family members and what they have taught you. Consider your early years. Did you "graduate" from the school of hard knocks? Did you have a bad experience doing something similar? Do you know someone or know someone who knows someone who has failed?

Did your parents often comment on your weight? Did they tell you that you were too skinny or needed to lose a few pounds? Parents, even with the best of intentions, often imprint things on their children's subconscious that have long-lasting effects. Armed with their desire to see you do well, they sometimes create the opposite or magnify an existing fear.

I have a good friend who decided to go to law school. When she announced this to her parents, her father suggested that she would not be happy being a lawyer and that she should consider another vocation where she would be happier. My friend was getting almost perfect grades in law school because she was following her passion, yet she dropped out halfway through because those seemingly innocuous comments were haunting her without her knowledge. This man who had given her so much truly good advice had torpedoed her heart's desire.

Another friend of mine struggled with success. He would do really well at work. But, as soon as the next promotion appeared on the horizon, my friend would find a way to ensure that he was passed over for the promotion. When we spoke about his childhood, he told me stories about mistakes that seemed like pretty normal childhood behavior to me. When I probed deeper, I discovered that his parents were never satisfied. He could bring home grades where he received a "B" in one class, but "A"s in every other subject, but his parents would focus on the "B." Worse, when he made a mistake, his parents often reminded him of something that he had lost because of the mistake. When he totaled the family's old station wagon, his father sadly told him that he was about to receive the title to the car, making it his. Is it any wonder that my friend consistently found ways to not quite measure up? His parents weren't abusing him. I'm quite sure that they were trying to help him be a better human. But, it backfired, badly and it took my friend well into his forties to understand this hidden fear of success. The good news is that once he did, his life almost immediately changed for the better.

EXERCISE: FUEL TO CHANGE

Although difficult, make a list of your greatest failures. Include how you felt and how the people around you reacted to your failure.

Also, make a list of your greatest victories. Perhaps you received a trophy or certificate. Or, maybe you always receive compliments on your lasagna?

How did you feel? How did you celebrate?

Armed with these two lists, let's move forward.

10

REFRAMING & REPORTING

To me, the first best step in putting fears to rest is to create some distance. I use two systems to accomplish this.

First, I use reframing. Whenever I discover a fear, I give it a physical shape. So, if I didn't have a driver's license because I was afraid of being in a car crash, I would create a picture of a crunched car. By the way, you can do this in your mind, but it becomes even more effective when you can find a picture or create a collage of the fear on a piece of paper.

Now that my fear is staring me in the face, I imagine it framed, like an artwork in a museum. Art is a wonderful medium because a painting, sculpture or other artwork is totally subject to the interpretation of the viewer. Two people can look at the same art piece and have completely different reactions. Likewise, the same person can view an artwork at two different times and have a different response to the art.

I can look at the physical "art" that demonstrates my fear in a physical form from a safe distance. I can return to it multiple times and probably have different reactions to the same fear.

In between viewings, I can also add knowledge. A college student who is studying art history develops a refined system for interpreting works of art that go beyond a simple visceral reaction. By studying politics, geography and life sciences, the student learns to view the art in the context in which it was created. Perhaps the artist was very poor, had no hands and used food scraps to create his pigments, applied by holding the brush in his teeth. Do you think they see the work differently with this new knowledge?

In your case, adding knowledge can come in different forms. If you are afraid to lose weight, you might study people who have lost significant weight and kept it off. What new habits did they employ to make it happen? You might read about difficult circumstances they faced overcame in order to get healthy. You might also study people who have failed at changing their body appearance and the reasons behind their failures.

Armed with this new knowledge, I'm guessing that your "art" will look different. In my car crash example, knowledge might come from studying statistics on how many drivers actually crash. I might also study crash test ratings. I might even talk to friends who have been in a crash to better understand how their accident happened and how they returned to driving after a crash.

By creating "art" from your fears, I expect that you will discover three things. First, the distance will help you look at the fear objectively. Second, turning your fear into a physical thing will help give your fear a face. Finally, adding knowledge will change the frame around your picture and how you view it.

Please understand that this is not a one and done exercise. Your subconscious in not going to change gears that easily. You will probably have to develop multiple art projects from a single fear before your subconscious will stand down.

The second technique I use involves a temporary vocational change, unless you are currently a television reporter. When you watch the local or national news, you will notice that the news anchors report information to you with little or no emotion. I have not seen a news anchor burst into tears as they report a fire where no one was hurt. However, I do see them deliver positive emotion when they report that no one was hurt in the fire because the family dog woke everyone up so they could escape.

Now take this news anchor skill set and apply it to your fears. Report your fear to yourself as if you are reporting a news story. It may seem silly, but trust me, it works. Actually, it is a bit silly. Imagine yourself standing in front of your bathroom mirror, reporting that you are overweight because you are afraid of being hurt again.

The key to reporting your fears is that you must do follow up reporting. "Jane only drank one Pepsi today as the pounds continue to fall off her body in anticipation of asking out that cute guy at the hardware store," sounds really funny when you hold a brush up like a reporter's microphone and try to maintain a somewhat serious expression. But, is it not better to laugh than to be afraid? And guess what? Laughter helps your subconscious receive the new programming you need to move forward because you are now attaching and anchoring a good feeling to losing weight.

Notice in the above updated reporting that I mentioned the pounds continuing to fall off? This is a good way to get comfortable with gratitude. I'm not telling my subconscious that I need to lose weight, because the Universe will honor my wish and continue to give me weight to lose. Instead, I am focusing on being grateful for what is ALREADY happening, even if I can't see it in the mirror or scale right away.

As I already mentioned, your subconscious is not going to lie down just because you tell it to. The advantage of my techniques is that they are more subtle. Your subconscious is slowly being molded into a calmer position where fears become cautions and then become assets.

Always be willing to ask yourself, "Is that really what drives my fear about…(fill in the blank)" Your subconscious knows the true answers and it will reveal them to you, but sometimes it takes a while, especially if the fear has been locked in place by deep pain or trauma. Be willing to dig around a bit, uncovering layers as they become available. You may also need to adjust your art or your reporting as you realize that what is driving a particular fear is not what you thought it was.

There are several feelings or emotions that can create misdirection in our fears. The most common is insecurity. Insecurity is also built and maintained in your subconscious, BUT insecurity is a fear masking a deeper fear. Worrying about a partner's infidelity, assuming they have been consistently faithful is often driven by a feeling that you aren't enough to keep your partner's attention. But, as you are digging deeper, you might learn or remember constant comments from your parents about your shortcomings. This is the kind of stuff you need to get to really change your future. If you don't dig deep, your changes will be superficial and short lived.

EXERCISE: FUEL TO CHANGE

Take your greatest failure and place it in a picture frame in your mind. You may need to draw a picture in your mind. Perhaps the "art" of losing your secure job is the image of homelessness. Walk back and forth in front of your "art" and consider it from different angles, like an art critic would. How does your fear look different from different angles?

Take your greatest fear and give it life. If you are afraid of another heartbreak, imagine a scene from a television show where one character has just had their heart broken. But, instead of letting the "actors" in your mind speak, take on the role of a news reporter. Imagine yourself reporting on this "breaking news." "This is Bob, live on the scene of Bob's heart break during his junior year of high school. There is carnage everywhere." Have some fun with this, but thoroughly report the story, including interviewing "you."

11

SPLIT TESTING AND LITTLE VICTORIES

Think about a business opportunity. What is the worst-case scenario if you start and fail? Because we are brought up in a negative world, we tend to think the worst imaginable consequences. "Oh boy, if I fail, my family and I will be living in a refrigerator box under the highway." This is not true at all. If you really think it through you would find that if you happened to get into a business that failed, the worst case scenario is that you will lose a great deal of money, which stinks, but it's not the end of the world, no one is going to die. The reality is that you will have to get a job and pay back the debt that you incurred. At the opposite spectrum, what if your business was wildly successful?

When I coach my clients who are making a transition from employee to business owner, I encourage them to think like the Wright Brothers. The Wright brothers defied the law of gravity by understanding why things do not fly and then concentrated and focused on all the ways they can make something fly. If they only thought about why things don't fly, we all would be vacationing every summer very close to where we live.

A friend related this story to me. When he was first starting in sales, my friend quickly realized that focusing on closed deals was very frustrating, if not downright demoralizing. By only focusing on the end zone, he was dreading the time in between deals, even though he liked what he was doing.

Instead of accepting these feelings, my friend chose instead to create "little victories." In his case, this meant that he needed to dissect the sales process from a deal backwards to his initial contact with a prospect. He noted that there were several milestones along the way that were most likely to produce the result he wanted. Some of these steps included a first face-to-face or telephone interaction with the person making the buying decisions, being allowed to see the businesses' current equipment (he was selling copiers), etc.

My friend also recognized that he needed to create a reward system for himself. He bought bags of those mini candy bars and left them in a cooler in his car. Each time he created a little victory, he stopped what he was doing, returned to his car and slowly enjoyed one of those little candy bars.

Within three months, this guy was the most successful salesperson in the office and was quickly promoted where he could then teach his methods to other salespeople.

Your brain, at a chemical level, will work for more good or it will work for more bad. Our friend Charlie Brown was programmed to work for bad, to the point that his brain would beg for a failure. When you have a life victory, dopamine is released into your brain, lifting your spirits. If you create little victories and stop to celebrate each one, your brain will crave success, supporting the very manifesting you are already doing.

With fear, there are often little victories to be had, too. If you were deathly afraid of flying, the mere walk into an airport terminal might create sweaty palms, a rapid heartbeat and other physical symptoms of anxiety. But, if you decide that walking into the terminal is a little victory and you keep trying until you can view the terminal like any other building, you will be one step closer to overcoming your fear. Perhaps the next step would be to have lunch in the terminal. Another might be going to a small airport and asking a private pilot to allow you to sit in his plane on the ground while he shows you all of the instruments and airplane parts that make flying safe. You can have him explain basic aerodynamics that makes flying planes safe. You may feel better once you learn that if a plane engine did have a problem the machine would not just drop out of the air. Actually, a jumbo jet can cruise for 125 miles with absolutely no engine power. For me, that is comforting to know.

But, is this person afraid of flying or afraid of crashing or perhaps not being in control and having the ability to pull over like in an automobile? The answer will drive their framing and reporting and will also probably adjust their little victories.

Alternately, they might not really know what they are afraid of. By using little victory steps, this person can better isolate their fear. I call this split testing.

If you aren't exactly sure what is behind a fear, take a couple different paths towards whatever you are afraid of and see which one creates the strongest physical reaction in you. If you are trying to diagnose why you are afraid of buying a franchise business, attend a franchising show. But, also spend some time at a homeless shelter. Which one makes you more uncomfortable? Whichever one it is, that's where the framing, reporting and little victories pathways should be aimed.

Split testing different paths is also directly in line with your manifesting. You aren't being distracted by your fears, but rather seeking knowledge to help you uncover and conquer them and the Universe will help you along the way by placing lessons in your path to reinforce that you are on the right track.

EXERCISE: FUEL TO CHANGE

Make a list of little victories you can celebrate as you move away from your fears and towards your dreams.

Make a list of rewards you will give yourself at each milestone.

12

OPENING CLOSED DOORS

When one door closes, another one opens. This is a popular adage. However, many people are afraid of what's behind the new door. Embrace change. Deepak Chopra says, "Change is the only constant. Holding on to anything is like holding your breath, if you hold on long enough, you'll suffocate." The flow of life as we know it is change. Although we say that things are boring and it's the same old routine, actually no two days are alike. For one thing, the weather is different, even if only a few degrees.

As a participant in this thing called earth, you're already used to change. Why do you resist it? The short answer is: we are lazy. Change, a lot of the time, means we have to think. Be uncomfortable. However, it's important to note that when we're uncomfortable, that's when we are learning and growing. That's why they call it growing pains!

Many people are concerned about making a mistake or

looking foolish. The interesting thing is that there are no mistakes, only different experiences. We tend to attach labels for situations based on experiences of folks who have gone before us and only knew how to operate from fear.

They would tell you to get a good job, be stable. Even if you're unhappy, they will say, at least you can pay your bills. Is paying bills why you're on this planet? I don't think that's what our forefathers had in mind when they wrote that in this country you have the right to pursue happiness. Freedom to pay bills is not why Columbus came to America.

So how do you do it, how do you live? If you take a leap of faith to make a left turn, dormant forces, fate will come to your aid. When you make a bold move destiny will have your back.

13

DECISION TIME

Only those who dare to fail greatly can ever achieve greatly.

–Robert F. Kennedy

Your life is merely evidence of the decisions or choices you made up to that point in your life. Decision time is the pivotal point in life that can create great rewards. And to not make a decision is a decision in itself.

Yet, more often than not, we put decisions off. If they can change our life, why wait? Most people wait because of UFO's in their life. I'm talking about Unidentified Flying Objects. I am speaking of the trifecta of villains of change.

The trifecta of villains are:

UNCERTAINTY – Most people think that they have to be certain about an outcome before making a decision. The truth is that decisions must be made based on the greatest probability. If you wait for certainty, it will never happen. This is why great leaders are highly paid – they make the tough decisions.

FEAR – Fear of failure. In reality, the only failure is to NOT make a decision. You will find that once you make a decision, the rest is easy. Decisions are never wrong; they just lead to different outcomes and experiences along your journey.

OVERWHELM – Our world forces people to make decisions faster and faster all the time. Amid faxes, emails and voicemails people expect an instantaneous answer, which gives us stress, and pressure all of the time. Often, our decision is to just shut down and not make a decision at all. For important life decisions - take the time to weigh all of the facts.

Making decisions, changing your life and going out of your comfort zone takes practice. You're using mental muscle that has not been used or is seldom called upon in your everyday life.

Here are some tips to help you make a proper business decision. Make decisions based on the specifics of your investigation, not hearsay, laymen's opinions or emotion. Facts will help you to focus on the outcome and help you to identify the results that will benefit you the most in the long run.

All-important decisions must be made on paper. If you attempt complex decisions in your head you will get the "loop effect" and you'll go crazy.

Be clear about your outcome, WHAT you want and WHY you want it.

All decisions are based on probability or risk/reward. That's why the decision making process is so powerful. Be sure that the decision is in line with your core values.

Not making a timely decision could indicate that you are not mentally prepared to make a big life change. In the final analysis, do not ignore your "gut!"

Whether you are trying to decide between two cars or two houses or two States to live in, you will find the following six steps to be a useful process to help you get to the verdict:

1. OUTCOMES

What results do you want from this change?

Why do you want these results?

How will they make your life different?

2. OPTIONS

If not this change then what will be the same or be different?

3. CONSEQUENCES

What are the upsides and downsides of both your current situation and the new possible situation?

What are you gaining or giving up with each option?

Is the decision in line with your core values and personal mission statement?

4. EVALUATE

Weigh the possible outcome of each option.

Evaluate each upside and downside.

In terms of meeting your goals, how important is each upside/downside?

What is the probability that each of the upsides or downsides with occur?

What is the benefit or consequence of each of these upsides and downsides if they actually happened?

Does this decision jeopardize my integrity?

5. MITIGATE

Review the downside consequences for each option.

Brainstorm ways to eliminate or reduce the cons.

6. RESOLVE

Based on the most probable outcomes of each option, select the option that provides the greatest certainty that you will meet your desired goals.

Select the best option and commit to making it work.

Resolve that no matter what happens, this option will give you a win.

Take the next step to put your selection to work and take action. You know your outcome- now it's time to make the plans to get to your dreams!

Making a Decision is Sometimes Simple

I believe that we are all born with two brains. One is the brain in our head; the other is the one in our gut.

The brain in our head is only as old and reliable as man has been on this earth. As opposed to the brain in our gut. This brain, while mostly ignored, is as old as the universe. Billions of years, actually infinite years. Although most commonly ignored, our gut brain or gut reaction is so much more reliable than our traditional brain.

Our traditional brain operates from data provided by other traditional brains. The Universe or God provides our gut reaction. Hmm, what would you trust?

Have you ever purchased a house? Before going into see the home, you probably sat with a great real estate agent who showed you pictures and stats of properties that looked awesome for you and your family. The amount of bedrooms and baths is great, love the garage, love that the house faces a certain direction and more than anything, the price is affordable. You then take a ride out to see the house. You're excited; this could be where you will raise your kids. You get there and the curb appeal is perfect. You would be proud to show your friends your new home. Then you walk through the threshold and all the positive energy gets suck right out of you! What happened? You can't quite put your finger on it or articulate it, but something is just not right.

Could this be the Universe or God telling you this is not the place you need to be? Only you can tell.

Have you ever walked into a room and felt heaviness in the environment. The energy is stagnant. Maybe you sense a negative vibration. Some people are sensitive to these types of feeling or they are able to detect energy patterns in an environment. Actually, we all can. We just need to turn off or tune out interfering energy. Maybe people are talking about you and sending negative poison energy toward you. You can feel it when you walk into a room, can't you?

Cooking Rice

When I get to the point of making big life decisions I am reminded of an old Chinese proverb that my mentor, Jeff Elgin, shared with me that helps me to avoid UFO's." The proverb is: "Talk doesn't cook rice."

Often we spend so much time talking or thinking or planning that we never get around to acting on our intentions. We get stuck in the quagmire of doubt, perfectionism and distractions, and that stops us from moving forward. So, to help propel you from inaction to accomplishment, focus on what's really important. Here are some tips to help you get cooking.

1. Don't over-think. It's good to have a clear picture of where you're going or why, but too much thinking can be paralyzing. Don't over-think, just do.

2. Forget perfection. Perfectionism is the enemy of action. Kill it, immediately. You can't let perfect stop you from doing. You can turn a bad draft into a good one, but you can't turn no draft into a good draft. So get going.

3. Don't mistake motion for action. A common mistake. A fury of activity doesn't mean you're doing anything. When you find yourself moving too quickly, doing too many things at once, this is a good reminder to stop. Slow down. Focus.

4. Focus on the important. Clear the distractions. Pick the one most important thing you must do today, and focus on that. Exclusively. When you're done with that, repeat the process.

5. Move slowly, consciously. Be deliberate. Action doesn't need to be done fast. In fact, that often leads to mistakes, and while perfection isn't at all necessary, neither is making a ridiculous amount of mistakes that could be avoided with a bit of consciousness.

6. Take small steps. Biting off more than you can chew will also kill the action. It creates overwhelm. Just take smaller steps. Little tiny blows that will eventually break down that mountain. Darren Hardy, publisher of Success Magazine calls this the "compound effect". This notion is so powerful, Darren wrote an entire book about it called, *"The Compound Effect."*

7. Negative thinking gets you nowhere. Seriously, stop doing that. Self doubt? The urge to quit? Telling yourself that it's OK to be distracted and that you can always get to it later? Squash those thoughts. Well, OK, you can be distracted for a little bit, but you get the idea. Positive thinking, as corny as it sounds, really works. It's self-talk, and what we tell ourselves has a funny habit of turning into reality.

8. Meetings aren't action. This is a common mistake in management. They hold meetings to get things done. Meetings, unfortunately, almost always get in the way of actual doing. Stop holding those meetings!

9. Talking (usually) isn't action. Well, unless the action you need to take is a presentation or speech or something. Or you're a television broadcaster. But usually, talking is just talking. Communication is necessary, but don't mistake it for actual action.

10. Planning isn't action. Sure, you need to plan. Do it, so you're clear about what you're doing. Just do it quickly, and get to the actual action as quickly as you can.

11. Reading about it isn't action. You're reading an book about action. Ironic, I know. But let this be the last one for now. Get to work!

14

FEAR OR FAITH?

The entire world lives from the base of fear. Fear of loss, fear that there is not enough, in addition to fear of trivial matters such as traffic, tardiness or, if my neighbor is stealing from me?

Emotion and thought attract like circumstances. If you fear that your country will be attacked, it will be. If you fear you will not get a parking spot, you won't. Of you think you're being cheated out of something, you lose.

If you dare to let go and have faith in God, fear and stress go away. If you have faith that you will put down your guns and bury your missiles, your enemy will have no reason to attack you. Take away the reason, live from a place of love and your enemy will have to go somewhere else. Put away the fear that your friends are talking about you and they will have nothing to talk about. Live from a place of love.

In the moment of your decision you either stop energy or promote flow. If you are given the wrong change at a store in your favor and you accept it you have then stopped the flow of money back to you in favor of a few bucks. Or, if you return the money and go with the flow, you open the floodgates.

If you receive wrong change in the other person's favor, point it out. But don't take it personally. Even if the person is doing it consciously, it is not about you. It is about them and their lack attitude. If you think the universe plan to get you stuck in traffic, if you think it's about you, you will continue to stop the flow...of traffic.

Choose love, do the right thing. Let go of fear, worry expectation and judgment and you will be in love, have no stress ad be part of the energy of the universe.

The road of life

The road of life if paved smoothly. If you choose consciously or subconsciously to be a pothole you will cause a slow down of energy to you. In life if you choose to be a beautiful rock formation or a great tree, people will pass by and admire you. They will pass good energy to you. People will bring their friends to see you and enjoy you. No one ever goes back to see a pothole. Actually, people will take a different route just to avoid you.

Choose to live with Faith. Choose love.

15

SUMMARY

So, there you have it. You are educated as to the foundation of fears and armed with the best tools for displacing those fears. My hope is that hearing my and Gina's story, as well as the experiences of others, will give you a laugh, but also that it will inspire you as you realize that EVERYONE is capable of living the life they want, on their terms.

I am thankful that you chose to take the precious time to read my book, and I hope you feel blessed and accepting of all of the success that will now be coming your way.

Best Wishes.

Tom Scarda, April 2014

SUGGESTED READING, SOURCES AND INSPIRATIONS

7 Habits of Highly Effective People by Steven R. Covey (Copyright Simon & Schuster)

A New Earth, Awaking to Your Life's Purpose by Eckhart Tolle (Copyright 2005, Plum Printing)

As a Man Thinketh by James Allen (Copyright 1902)

Change Your Thoughts – Change Your life, Living the Wisdom of the Tao by Dr. Wayne W. Dyer (Copyright 2007, Hay House)

Conversations with God, An Uncommon Dialogue, Book 1 by Neale Donald Walsch (Copyright 1995, Hampton Roads Publishing)

Dare to Dream, Beat The Odds and Win Personal Success by Florence Litttauer (Copyright 1991

<u>Daring Greatly</u> by Brene' Brown, Ph.D., LMSW (Copyright 2012, Gotham Books)

<u>Enjoy Every Sandwich, Living Each Day as if It Were Your Last</u> by Lee Lipsenthal, M.D (Copyright 2011, Crown Publishing)

<u>Every Day a Friday</u> by Joel Osteen (Copyright 2011, Hachette Book Group)

<u>Experience Your Good Now! Learning to Use Affirmations</u> by Louise L. Hay (Copyright 2010, Hay House)

<u>Feel The Fear and Do It Anyway, Dynamic Techniques for turning Fear, Indecision, and Anger into Power, Action and Love</u> by Susan Jeffers, Ph.D. (Copyright 1987, 2007 Ballantine Books)

<u>How to Win Friends and Influence People</u> by Dale Carnegie (Copyright 1936, Simon & Shuster)

<u>Leveraging the Universe, 7 Steps to Engaging Life's Magic</u> by Mike Dooley (Copyright 2011, Atria Paperback)

<u>Push</u> by Chalene Johnson (Copyright 2012, Rodale)

Rich Dad, Poor Dad by Robert T. Kiyosaki (Copyright 1999, Techpress)

Secrets of the Millionaire Mind, Mastering the Inner Game of Wealth by T. Harv Eker (Copyright 2005, Harper Collins)

Sometimes You Win, Sometimes You Learn, Life's Greatest Lessons are Gained From our Losses by John C. Maxwell

The 4-Hour Work Week by Timothy Ferris (Copyright 2007, Crown Publishing)

The Book of Secrets, Unlocking the Hidden Dimensions of Your Life by Deepak Chopra (Copyright 2004, Crown Publishing)

The Choice by Og Mandino (Copyright 1972, Bantam)

The Compound Effect by Darren Hardy (Copyright 2010, Success Media)

The Four Agreements by Miguel Angel Ruiz, M.D. (Copyright 1997, Amber-Allen Publishing)

The Gifts of Imperfection, Let Go of Who You Think You're Supposed to Be and Embrace Who You Are by Brene' Brown, Ph.D., LMSW (Copyright 2010, Hazelden)

The Law of Attraction: The Basics of the Teachings of Abraham by Esther Hicks and Jerry Hicks (Copyright 2006, Hay House)

The Magic of Thinking Big by David J. Schwartz, Ph. D (Copyright 1959, Prentic-Hall)

The Power of Positive Thinking by Normal Vincent Peale (Copyright 1953 Prentice-Hall)

The Richest Man in Babylon by George S. Clason (Copyright 1955, Signet)

The Science of Getting Rich by Wallace Wattles (Copyright 1910)

The Seat of the Soul by Gary Zukav (Copyright 1989, Fireside)

The Spontaneous Fulfillment of Desire, Harnessing the Infinite Power of Coincidences by Deepak Chopra (Copyright 2003, Three Rivers Press)

Success Magazine, Darren Hardy, Publisher and Editor

Think and Grow Rich by Napolean Hill (Copyright 1960, Highroads Media)

Unlimited Power by Anthony Robbins (Copyright 1986, Ballantine Books)

ABOUT THE AUTHOR

Tom Scarda is known as a dynamic speaker, motivator and author and counted as someone who is not content with a status quo life. More than two decades ago, searching for his inner drive, Tom left the mainstream world of college and submerged himself in the motorcycle underworld in the lower eastside of Manhattan. This made his mother worry. It was the first time Tom chose uncertainty.

After four years of motorcycle gang life in NYC, Tom obtained a respectable job as a Metropolitan Transit Authority - New York City Subway Train Conductor. Working quickly up the ranks, he became a manager responsible for train movement in the largest municipal train yard in the Western Hemisphere.

Realizing that civil service was not the answer for his creative side, he gave up many promotions and even a pension, to pursue his dreams of business ownership. This made his mother worry. In 2000, he bought into a national smoothie franchise company. Tom built his franchise into three units, sold it in 2005 and semi-retired at the age of 41. Now, on a daily basis, Tom inspires people to live outside of their comfort zone and choose uncertainty over unhappiness.

Tom's mantra is; "There are no wrong turns, just different experiences." However some folks just move in circles. Mr. Scarda helps folks navigate out of their endless loop and toward their God-given mission. Everyone has a passion sleeping within his or her soul. Tom's mission is to help people harvest their own passion for the betterment of the world.

Tom lives on Long Island with his wife Gina, their two children and two dogs. Tom does not ride motorcycles any longer. He graduated to flying planes. He said, "The way I measure risk is, if it's something that makes a mother worry, it's for me!"

28355589R00074

Printed in Great Britain
by Amazon